I WANT TO BE A...

WRITER

DOUG BRADLEY

PowerKiDS press.

New York

Published in 2023 by The Rosen Publishing Group, Inc.
29 East 21st Street, New York, NY 10010

First Edition

Editor: Caitie McAneney
Book Design: Rachel Rising

Photo Credits: Cover, p.1 Quality Stock Arts/Shutterstock.com; pp. 4, 6, 8, 10, 12, 1, 16 ,18, 20 april70/Shutterstock.com; p. 5 Roman Samborskyi/Shutterstock.com; p. 7 fizkes/Shutterstock.com; p. 9 Rawpixel.com/Shutterstock.com; p. 11 metamorworks/Shutterstock.com; pp. 13, 15 GaudiLab/Shutterstock.com; p. 17 Oleksii Didok/Shutterstock.com; p. 19 Zephyr_p/Shutterstock.com; p. 21 https://commons.wikimedia.org/wiki/File:210120-D-WD757-2714_(50861221216).jpg.

Some of the images in this book illustrate individuals who are models. The depictions do not imply actual situations or events.

Library of Congress Cataloging-in-Publication Data
Names: Bradley, Doug.
Title: Writer / Doug Bradley.
Description: New York : PowerKids Press, 2023. | Series: I want to be a... | Includes glossary and index.
Identifiers: ISBN 9781725339972 (pbk.) | ISBN 9781725339996 (library bound) | ISBN 9781725339989 (6pack) |
ISBN 9781538385364 (ebook)
Subjects: LCSH: Authorship–Vocational guidance–Juvenile literature. | Authorship–Juvenile literature.
Classification: LCC PN151.B656 2023 | DDC 808.02–dc23

Manufactured in the United States of America

CPSIA Compliance Information: Batch #CSPK23. For Further Information contact Rosen Publishing, New York, New York at 1-800-237-9932.

CONTENTS

What Do Writers Do?

Writing is a great job if you like to **create**. Writers create new worlds through stories. Writers create beautiful **poems**. They create plays and movies that make people think. Some write for children, while others write for adults.

Where Do Writers Work?

Writers can work from anywhere in the world! They only need a piece of paper and a pen. Today, many writers use **laptops**. Laptops can be taken almost anywhere. Writers often write from an office, either at home or in a workplace.

Writing Fiction

Some writers create works of fiction. Fiction is something that's made up. Some writers create short stories. Others write longer fiction books, called novels. They think about who or what they want to write about. Then, they bring the story to life.

Writing Plays and Movies

Playwrights are writers who write plays. Plays are stories that take place live on stage. Screenwriters write movies. Both kinds of writers must decide what characters will say. They help bring a story to life on the stage or screen.

Writing Poetry

Poets are writers who create poems. Poems are often shorter than stories. Poems have a beat or flow to them, called rhythm. Poets must choose words that make their readers feel something. They might write about nature, feelings, or a person.

Writing to Teach

Writing that is based on something true is called nonfiction. Some nonfiction writers create books to teach readers something. They use facts. Writers called journalists write about the news, or what's happening in the world. They may write short pieces called articles.

Copywriting

Copywriters write things for companies. The company might want to sell a **product**. The copywriter can write about the product. Their writing might also be put on the product. Everything on the back of your cereal box was written by a copywriter!

How to Be a Writer

Some people learn to write just by writing and reading on their own. Some people go to **college** to be a writer. They might study one kind of writing closely, such as poetry or playwriting. They read many things to learn how to become a good writer.

Writers Make a Difference

If you love to read and write, a job as a writer might be perfect for you. You can make a difference as a writer. Amanda Gorman is a young poet who speaks at important events. Her poetry helps bring people together.

GLOSSARY

college: A school people can go to after high school.

create: To make something new.

laptop: A small computer that can be carried around.

poem: A piece of writing written in a special way to make people feel something.

product: Something made or grown that is offered for sale.

FOR MORE INFORMATION

BOOKS

Dennis, Elizabeth. *If You Love Books, You Could Be…* New York, NY: Simon Spotlight, 2020.

Kawa, Katie. *Amanda Gorman: Making a Difference with Her Words*. New York, NY: KidHaven Publishing, 2023.

WEBSITES

8 Things to Know About Amanda Gorman

storyworks.scholastic.com/pages/archives/articles/8-things-to-know-about-amanda-gorman.html
Discover fun facts about a famous young writer, Amanda Gorman.

Poetry Writing Lessons for Kids

www.poetry4kids.com/lessons/poetry-writing-lessons/
You can write a poem! Learn about different forms of poetry and how to write them.

INDEX